(Collection of Poetry)

by Marcos Cummings

BOOKS
ACADEMY
LEARNING LIFE FROM EVERY PAGE

Books Academy LLC
112 SW H K Dodgen Loop,
Temple, Texas 76504
Hotline: (254) 800-1189

Ordering Information:
Quantity sales. Special discounts are available on quantity purchases by corporations, associations, and others. For details, contact the publisher at the address above.

Printed in the United States of America.

ISBN-13:   Softcover   978-1-964929-83-5
                 eBook   978-1-964929-82-8

Library of Congress Control Number: 2024924811

Table of Contents

Everything you can do
If all I can do
If you can do better
Then else is there to do
But to wait a second and do something new
I tell you this, I can do it better than you
What can I do but tell you the truth
Yes, I can
No, you can't
If I can try I will do
What else can I do if I can't do better?
I think I can but can't
I know you won't, you cant
Yes, I can

Listen to me, heart
Can you hear words that I speak?
Can you understand what I'm saying?
Can you know what's about to break?
Should dance when you alone
Why should I listen to you when it hurt so bad?
Where should I go when time is alone?
My heart breaks when I'm sad
But it's heard by many

Real Brother

How to be true
How to be honorable
How to be strong
Leader
Friend
No foe
Or is it looks or reality
Is it business or hope?
What makes you strong willed?

Respect toward All

We need to respect our brothers and sisters
Honor one another
Love toward us all

Strength in Love

Love is an overcomer

Love is mighty

Love flows like the wind

Love is strong, it can destroy everything

Love can do all things

Love can grow into a butterfly

Life can be filled with love

Life can filled with hate and anger but through it all love wins

Love can overcome it all

Today love still grows even in bad situations

Do the Right Thing

Do what's right, be right
Listen to what's right
Be righteous
Speak in right tones right away, be right
Be kind toward people
All these are right but do it wisely
Be cool and be kind
Be able
Be smart
Be knowledgeable

Don't Give Up

Stay calm
Depend on what it is
What is said
Don't give up
Try hard to pull through
Listen to hard advice
Be careful, be true to yourself
Stay alert
Don't give in

World's Strongest

I'm Army strong
Tuff enough to get through
Can you keep up
Be tall, be wide
Be there when everybody notices
I'm strong because I believe
Strong enough to build lives
Pull through it all

Beautiful Church

How wonderful you are for love speaks of you
You are nice, are joyful
Your words were learned from righteousness
I believe that you are natural in your love
Your faith has kept you
Peace in our lives because of you
Faith is something that brings peace of mind
Honor is on your belt of armor
We speak of what is right and peaceable

Freedom

We need freedom, without that how can we live
With chains of discovery
Who can we trust, who can we live by
If everybody was bound up from freedom
If we are bound then how can we be free
Our freedom is everything to us
We can all learn from wars of freedom
Can I be free no without the truth of life
Mine is where freedom starts

Love

I love forever
I need you
That's what love could be if you try
Love also can be divine
It can be encouraging
Love can be strong and powerful
How can we grow without love
How can family be together without love
How can the earth sit still without love

The Will

I will keep going on
Safe is me
Strong is me
I will remain strong
My purpose is to continue on
Faith keeps me driving on
Understanding is what it's like
The will of a right man is doing what's right
The will

The Call

I am an American and I know I'm free
My duty to my country keeps together
My freedom keeps me calm
In knowing who I am
Faith in myself keeps me
Never keep a man down
Strength in numbers
Family is everything

Wisdom

What is wisdom?
Can wisdom stand by itself
Can wisdom stand still?
Can wisdom fall?
No
Wisdom can be strong when it hurts
Wisdom can be strong when times are hard

Being Yourself

I am an American and I know I'm free
My duty to my country keeps together
My freedom keeps me calm
In knowing who I am
Faith in myself keeps me
Never keep a man down
Strength in numbers
Family is everything

Africa
You are a beauty

That shines in the Hills
Dear Africa, your people are great
Africa, great and wonderful are you
I love the culture you are
I love the way you dance
Wisdom are your words that come from your elders

Love of My Culture

I love you with strength
Love with all respect, with all gentleness
My love for you will win you
Because you are free from evil
I believe we have overcome with love
My culture will survive
We will overcome
Justice will rise again
Peace shall come

Beauty in Everyone

We all are equal

Our beauty can look the same way

But how can you measure

Should we measure taste, style our being

How can we judge one another

By respectfully judging our hearts

We should love one another's peace

We all know not everyone is beautiful but how can we tell the difference

By showing respect for everyone.

Love All People

Everybody needs love, all of us

Love is a thing that cannot be hid

That can't be moved or stopped unless hate gets involved

Love can be powerful but we all need it

All people of the world need love

Another one loves one another

Put trust in love, if you can you shall be strong

Be strong and love even wins, it hurts

Real People

How to be real To be true

To be true to yourself and others

I say being real is something that

Honesty to people can be a powerful thing

Truth can be a thing that can hold tight in hard times
Lies fall and cry when time is up

Being true can be better than butter

Gain

Why do I want control?
Who can I gain?
Who can I stand, who can I regain
How can I stand?
Am I'm real enough
Can I stand enough bull? Will I gain respect?

USA

I'm proud to be an American

I'm strong in my faith

Never leave a man down

Stay strong to your belief, be faithful, respectful to your country

USA, proud to be

Freedom is a thing that cannot be measured

Honor towards those whose fight cannot be forgotten
The battle in war makes us free

We belong to a higher power

Our faith teaches us the true meaning of life

One

I'm one

I am a man

I'm a man that needs no one The man who fights for no glory I'm a man who battles for night In the shadows

When nobody's around

I fight final battles

When war is here I'm no one

The Will of the Lifelike Teeth

Why can I not move like this?

How can I be strong How can I be fair?

Who can you know?

Hard times come to destroy us But in due time we will overcome You stand the test of time

It's rough but somebody has to do it

Victory

Power of the Mind

Will comes from yourself
Your willpower can change everything
Mind is everything
The mind can affect it all
How can you think, see, move without it
The mind needs wisdom to grow
The mind needs knowledge to learn
Mind needs to be able to breathe

Dear Martin

Listen to me, a lot has changed

Ever since the rap in the 80s

Ever since the love respect between the two cultures

Their hate crimes and evil between the two be things been a lot better

There's been war, new evil

There's been a new outspoken man of God, his name is Bishop Jakes

Life's been good for the most part

Shadow of a Doubt

Why doubt's hold be strong

Be there for someone Don't give up

Don't quiet

Hold on and be strong, don't doubt yourself unless you know you are wrong

Don't doubt unless you are not sure, then it's ok

Don't doubt

At least try not to, be strong

Powerful Women

Women, you are bold
You are brave
There's nothing next to you
To all cultures your beauty is wonderful
You are very awesome
You are a great thing that is not to hide
We love you for your ways and your style

A Brotherly Love

You can't compare a love from your brother

Love that never leaves

Love that can't bend

Love that you can't find in others Love that you need to hold on to You need the love of your family Love is worth finding

Will of Men

Will you change will you grow
How often will you inspire
Will you go far?
How old are you
Can you create things that are spacious?
Can you determine what's right
How can you, will you, or let you

Dear X

What you been doing
Be brave out there
Be bold, be golden
Be the legend you can be
Strength is in love and the beauty of it
Your family culture at Kedesha needs you

Jessica

Ex-wife
Listen to me, Marcos, I know you are there
Where you are at
I know what you are listening to
I love you so
Our kid just turned 9 years
And life for me is ok
And I know that you ok, that we ok

Killing Me

Will you miss me
Will you love me
Will you lose me
Life for me can be a hush
But don't get mad at me when life hurts
I love you but don't take me away from you
I need you not but I like
Kill me if you can
Take me by storm if you can

Power to the People

Grow in the will of life
Power to the people who go through
Power to the people will survive
People who don't give up unless they have to
People who are everyday heroes
Life is good toward those who try
People who do respect others and love one another

Old-school New-schools' History

Have favor that retro
Are you into the old lee
Or are you into the new
Like Generation x or y
Or more like rap or rock
Really me, I'm a neutral
So you see if you are a convict fan or a zero fan
Then you are just a fan
But to me like to rock the show

The Will to Live

Got to get stronger, better, real

Can't give up, got to get better

Got go pro

Better luck with me in battle than with them

Got to survive the hard times

Better when we get going

Don't give up, I might make it

Strength in Faith

We believe that everything's going to be ok

We know that God is true

We know that everything is not an absolute

I believe because I know it's true

Without it I would not get stronger

Faith means everything but not all things

Love My Culture

I love the good, the bad

The battle within

Good days, the bad days

Life goes on but my culture will still be there

Culture teaches a lot about a person

Culture can express itself

I love the way we are, how we speak

Our slang, our walk, our move

I love our people, our enduring spirit

We are a strong culture that mostly lives by faith

Call of Duty

My mission is to be there for one another
Duty is to never leave a man behind
My life is to keep together
Keep the call
Die for my country
Die for my fellow men, die for freedom
I know that all I have to do to keep up
Duty call for a man who is devoted

Love One Another

I love you, honey

I can't tell her the truth

Why she needs to know because I have your child
Honey, I'm taking out the trash

Well, you know what, I guess you need to go I will make
you fade away

Listen, you had this baby, you need to take care of it

I thought you loved me, Nate

Well, honey, our 7-year-old wants to talk to you

African

You are a strong people who know for
I like the way you are
My faith stands with you
You are wonderfully made
Great are you, will be to might
Your natural look is beautiful

Beautiful Church

You love and are righteous, you are great
Wonderful are your ways, love is your shield
I like to think your holy ways come from up above
You are sweeter than a honeycomb
Your ways are true and mighty, your will is strong

One

We are one united
We are people who are nomads
Are we strong because we are one?
Really we are nothing without ourselves
But truth be told that we are more than our own
What can we do but be one
Can we fight alone, no
We can hide alone
Fight for our own
Moving on

Fighting Temperature

I raise my voice for my cry
I fight the best
I grab a weapon when I die
I fight the good fight when I lie
When I die I can't move
I fight with heat in my bones
When I fight the storm breaks
When I fight we give up
Only time will tell the truth about my fighting temp

Battle beyond the Whales

(Jessica and Marcos: X-mon-key-nia)
Be strong, don't give up
Put it all in you
Don't let out
Don't give up
Be strong in one another, Father said
Work hard for what you want
Jessica, you have a little girl
Marcos, you have a new baby, be wise
Marcos, love your wife, the battle is getting old
Jessica, your life will increase in measure

Dear Hunter Guy-u

Our final battle is about to begin

Get ready for the games

If you can't win then I will, MarcosX

Ok, let me tell you when we battle don't hold nothing back

Give it your all

Getting stronger, better, wiser

Be there or be square

Aren't you ready for this, man

www.ingramcontent.com/pod-product-compliance
Lightning Source LLC
Chambersburg PA
CBHW051336120626
46547CB00016B/2563